The Church—Maintained in Truth

Hans Küng

The Church—
Maintained in Truth

A THEOLOGICAL MEDITATION

SCM PRESS LTD

St. Paul's Clifton
Bray Library

Translated by Edward Quinn from the German
Kirche – gehalten in der Wahrheit?
copyright © 1979 by Benziger Verlag
Zurich, Einsiedeln, Cologne

Why I Remain a Catholic copyright © 1980 by Hans Küng

Translation copyright © 1980 by The Seabury Press, Inc.

All rights reserved. No part of this publication may be
reproduced, stored in a retrieval system, or transmitted,
in any form or by any means, electronic, mechanical,
photocopying, recording or otherwise, without the prior
permission of the publisher, SCM Press Ltd.

334 01939 7

First published in Britain 1980 by
SCM Press Ltd
58 Bloomsbury Street   London   WC1B 3QX

Typeset in the United States of America
and printed in Great Britain by
Billing and Sons Ltd
Guildford and Worcester

Contents

Preface

Why should there be a Church in the third millennium and even later? Why should its truth not ultimately come to an end once and for all? Why should the Church remain indefinitely in the truth? Is there to be a Church perpetually maintained in truth, despite all errors?

These are questions to which an answer will be presented here. It will not take the form of a "critical reflection"; it will not be yet another critique of the atheists' prognoses of an early end to religion, Christianity, and Church. It is meant to be a "theological meditation" in the light of the Christian message itself, making intelligible as far as possible in concrete terms the persistence of the Church in truth despite all errors and considering fully the numerous practical consequences. We venture to hope that it will help to create a new awareness of the power of Christian truth by which the Church has always lived and—we trust—will continue to live also in the future.

HANS KÜNG

Chapter 1

Maintained in Truth

No Extrapolation

Futurologists "extrapolate": from developments at the present time they draw conclusions about the still unknown future. Cannot the future of the Church also be extrapolated, projected in advance, in the light of the present? Can it not be predicted more or less exactly, from the history of the Church up to now, that there will be a Church also in the third millennium and even later?

Certainly the negative prophecies of Feuerbach, Marx, Nietzsche, and Freud have not been fulfilled. There is as yet no sign of an end of Christianity, a fading away of religion, a death of God. And faith in progress and science, disseminated in both East and West, which claimed as a substitute religion to solve all the problems of man and society, has meanwhile run into a crisis of its own and frequently turned into hostility against science and technology.

At the same time sociologists of religion are pointing

to the continually surprising, persistent vitality of the great religions, which are much older than any of the political systems: they cannot be expected to die out in the foreseeable future. Judaism and Islam, for instance, have displayed an amazing capacity for renewal in our time. Continually surprising also is the new vitality of Christianity as it finds expression in numerous initiatives to cope with world problems (racial equality, world peace, social justice) which, despite all failures, are repeatedly taken by the Christian churches and by individual Christians. Hence it is undoubtedly possible to extrapolate some trends from the history of the Church up to now, even though extrapolations by religious sociology are more in danger than others of failing to allow for the element of surprise in future happenings and of being no more than "prognoses of the past."

But, despite everything, looking at the situation as a whole, who would venture from the past two millennia of the Church to extrapolate an entire third? And who would promise in particular a steady, unrestricted continuity (perenniality), indestructibility (indefectibility), or—if it is not misunderstood as referring to individual propositions—inerrancy (infallibility) of the Church? For who knows? Perhaps science, technology, and rational enlightenment may yet make possible and even bring about a fulfilled, contented life without belief in God, rendering superfluous both Christianity and churches. Who would venture to prophesy about these things?

No, it is not possible to extrapolate indestructibility for the Church. Nor should there be any attempt to do so. For the indestructibility of the Church, its main-

tenance in truth, can be meaningfully asserted only as a
truth of faith. That is, Christians are confident that there
is a living God and that in the future this God will also
maintain their believing community in life and in truth.
Their confidence is based on the promise given with
Jesus of Nazareth: he himself is the promise in which
God's fidelity to his people can be read. How is this to
be understood?

A Truth of Faith

If we want to provide an adequate theological justification of the indestructibility of the Church today, it cannot be done in textbook fashion in biblicist-fundamentalist terms with the aid of an odd text or two, as
if at least in the Bible individual propositions were a
priori infallible. No, the Bible is not like the Koran, a
compendium of infallible propositions dictated by God
or by an angel, to be understood literally and observed
strictly, including the prohibition of alcoholic drink, the
veiling of women, and cutting off the hand of a thief.
The Bible is a collection of human documents which are
meant to bear witness in human weakness, limitation,
and frailty to God's word and deed. The indestructibility of the Church can be given adequate theological
justification only if it is supported not by individual
biblical texts but by *the Christian message as a whole*. As
a believer I can rely on its call, even though one or
another line of Scripture is uneven, even though one or
another proposition reflects the message only obscurely,
with some distortion, or perhaps fails entirely to reflect
it. God writes straight, even on crooked lines. And because of the crooked, very human lines, literary and fac-

tual criticism is unavoidable for a modern understanding of the Bible.

But again, what is not contained in a single proposition, but the basic conviction running through all the
New Testament writings, in fact the Christian message
itself, is:

- that the historical Jesus of Nazareth is more than
  merely one of the prophets, is not simply different
  from other prophets;
- that in him God's ultimate, decisive call, God's definitive truth about himself and man, found expression;
- that Jesus was and is therefore rightly called the true
  Lord, God's word made flesh, the way, the truth, and
  the life;
- that for believers—allowing for all genuine progress
  and all development and involvement—he cannot be
  surpassed or replaced by any new Lord, any other
  word, any better truth.

This is the message of faith of those believers who
with good reasons first committed themselves to him—
the one who was crucified and raised to life by God—
and who for their part want to provoke faith and hitherto have repeatedly provoked faith. Obviously I can
reject this provocation; I can say no. Faith is a free decision which presupposes open-mindedness, a readiness
to believe. And the less ordinary and banal, the higher
and more meaningful, the truth is, so much more open-
mindedness, so much more readiness, is required, even
though faith itself is by no means a blind and irrational,
but a justified and intelligent faith.

Since for believers Jesus is the decisive call of God,
his final word, his definitive revelation, from time im-

memorial the conviction of the believing community
has been:

- that God will always continue to find faith through
  this Jesus Christ;
- that consequently there will always continue to be
  human beings who come to believe in him;
- that there will always continue to be also a community
  of believers, that is, a Church of Jesus Christ in the
  broadest sense of the term.

Here then something fundamental has become clear.
Faith in the indestructibility of the Church—that is, in
its being maintained in truth—is related primarily to
the whole Church as believing community. It is not
primarily related to certain ecclesiastical institutions or
authorities, which for the most part did not exist at all
or did not exist in this form from the beginning and
need not exist or need not exist in this form forever.

Thus not only has the plane of institutions and authorities been penetrated but also that of propositional
truths, in order—if necessary through very varied statements—to point to one and the same reality which lies
behind the individual statements and alone gives them
their truth. It is only in the light of this reality, lying
behind all talk of faith, which was laid open by God
through Jesus for a community of faith, that the invitation to faith can actually be justified. To commit oneself
to this reality, to rely on the indestructibility of this
faith and this believing community, undoubtedly involves a risk, a venture. Faith cannot be "proved" in the
same way as other things are proved; it is a matter of
trust, naturally of reasonable trust. If someone has to
cope with the reality of God, he cannot have the assur-

ance that is provided by ordinary reality. But this very risk, the adventure of faith, involves a hope. Faith is related to a future still to be realized, but already inaugurated. When human beings have to cope with the reality of God, faith can provide a certainty which infinitely surpasses all banal, ordinary security.

Despite All Errors

This hope of the believing community in its future finds expression in various texts of Scripture, which are repeatedly cited in this connection by both Catholic and Protestant theologians as "classical" texts: "The powers of death shall not prevail against it" (Mt 16:18); "I am with you always, to the close of the age" (Mt 28:20); "And he [the Father] will give you another Counselor, to be with you for ever, even the Spirit of truth" (Jn 14:16–17); "The church of the living God, the pillar and bulwark of the truth" (1 Tim 3:15).

It is notable however that these "classical" statements about the Church and truth do not a priori exclude errors either of certain persons or in certain statements. On the contrary, the many failures and errors of men are continually taken for granted in the Bible from Genesis to Revelation. Only too often—even with the patriarchs and Moses, with the judges, kings, and prophets, and finally also with Peter and the apostles— these failures and errors are clearly demonstrated to us.

There are of course those who ask: If in faith we accept an indestructibility (indefectibility) of the Church, why not accept in the same faith an infallibility on the part of certain authorities or in certain statements of faith? But the difference is obvious. In the original

Christian testimony, on which we are dependent for the definition of what is Christian, truth is promised to the Church, but inerrancy is not guaranteed to any ecclesiastical authorities either permanently or in certain cases. On the contrary, the very prototype of the disciple of Jesus, Simon Peter, whose faith in Jesus as the living Christ became fundamental, even a "rock," to the Church, even he continually fails. On one occasion Jesus tells him, "Get behind me, Satan" (Mk 8:33). In this very way Peter is the type, the symbol, of the Church: his faith "may not fail" (Lk 22:32), although he too even in decisive situations does not act in accordance with the truth of the gospel and has to be severely corrected by Paul (cf. Gal 2:11–15). That is, if truth is to be continually in the Church, this will not be because the members or at least certain members in certain situations do not make mistakes or because their liability to error is sometimes excluded by higher influence. The reason why truth remains in the Church is because, in the face of all human failings and mistakes, God's truth proves to be stronger and because the message of Jesus continually produces faith, so that Jesus remains in the community of believers and his Spirit constantly guides them afresh into the whole truth.

Yes, what is truth? "Truth" (Hebrew *'emet*, Greek *alētheia*) in the Old and New Testament means essentially more than true, or correct, propositions or statements. "Truth" in the biblical sense means fidelity, permanence, reliability: the absolutely reliable fidelity of the God of the Covenant to his word, to his promise, and so to us. This is the truth of God: the absolute fidelity and reliability of God in regard to humankind, of a God who does not deceive himself or us; who never becomes a liar, however often he is cheated; who never refuses fellowship, even though it is constantly broken; who does not allow those who lapse to fall away forever. It is from this truth, fidelity, and reliability of God that the believer and the believing community can, should, and may live.

Why then does the Church remain alive as a community of faith? Not because there is no threat to life, no fatal illness, within it. But because God keeps it alive, *despite* all infirmities and weaknesses, and constantly endows it with a new continuity (perenniality).

Why does the Church remain in grace? Not because it is itself steadfast and faithful. But because, *despite* all sin and guilt, God does not dismiss it from his favor and grace and constantly grants it a new indestructibility (indefectibility).

Why does the Church remain in truth? Not because there is in it no wavering or doubting, no deviation or going astray. But because God maintains it in truth, *despite* its doubts, misunderstandings, and errors, and constantly gives it a new inerrancy (infallibility).

For the clarification of the traditional theological terminology it should be noted that in the New Testament the terms "life," "grace," and "truth" mean the same reality in which knowing and loving, talk and action, and man's living assent in everything to God are combined. Thus the terms "perenniality," "indefectibility," and "infallibility" overlap. They too mean one and the same reality, but in theological usage they can be more closely defined in one way or another and distinguished from each other. Since the terms "indefectibility" and "perenniality" have been traditionally connected more with the "being" than with the "truth" of the Church, but since also the being of the Church depends on its truth, in our context we have made use of the term "indefectibility" (perenniality) while defining it more closely: *indefectibility*, indestructibility (not only in being but also) *in truth*. The term "indefectibility" is oriented less than the term "infallibility" to certain statements or authorities. Above all, it is not encumbered with the many misunderstandings attached to the term "infallibility." Consequently "indefectibility" or "indestructibility" is to be preferred for current usage. If then the term "indefectibility" (of the Church) is used as opposed to "infallibility" (of individual propositions or authorities), it means the fundamental permanence of the Church in truth, a permanence which is not suspended by individual errors. An indefectibility of the Church in truth is supported by the New Testament as a whole, but an infallibility of certain authorities or statements cannot be proved. Instead, we must speak of an indefectibility of the Church despite all fallibility on the part of its human authorities and statements.

Chapter 2

Guided by the Spirit

Jesus Christ as Truth, Way and Life

Talk of the Church being maintained, remaining, in truth sounds very theoretical. But everything depends on understanding its concrete meaning. *Two misunderstandings* must be rejected from the very outset. The concrete meaning may fail to appear, but it may also be overemphasized and then it will be self-destructive.

Against a defective concrete expression it must be said that what remains is not merely God. To say that God remains is more or less a tautology. What is meant here is that God's truth remains, not only in heaven but also on earth, that God's truth is therefore effective in the Church. In this sense it is the Church itself which is maintained and remains.

Against an excessively concrete expression it must be said, after all our reflections, that the Church's persistence in truth cannot be given expression in infallible propositions. A genuinely concrete form of persistence in truth must be conceived differently. It is not a question of the permanence of certain propositions, but again of the permanence of the Church itself in truth.

How can the fact of being maintained in truth be positively defined? From what has been said hitherto it should have become clear that, for the Church, it is not a question of abstract truth—"What is truth?"—but of *Christian* truth, the *truth of the gospel of Jesus Christ.*

Hence the *first* answer to our question is that, in the concrete, the Church is maintained in truth whenever *Jesus himself* and not some other secular, political, or clerical figure *remains the truth* for the individual or the community. Jesus does not simply know or tell the truth. He personifies, he is the truth that leads to life. But he remains the truth for the individual and the community not simply because he is known, recognized, and acknowledged as the truth but because we live by the truth that he is: so that this Jesus—his message, his behavior, his lot—in the concrete existence of the individual and the believing community, is the orientation and the standard for relationships both to one's fellows and to human society, as also to God himself.

From this the *second* answer follows immediately, that the Church is maintained quite concretely in the truth of Jesus Christ not only where the right words are produced but wherever *discipleship is fully realized in practice:* wherever, that is, Jesus is not only proclaimed and believed but imitated and given living expression in a spirit of faith. For believing in him means committing oneself trustfully to him. And this again means participating quite practically in him and in his way, following my own way of life (and every person has his own way) in accordance with his guidance, in order in this way to reach true life through his living truth. He himself then is our way of salvation and way of life to God. He himself is the answer in regard to the right way, the permanently valid truth, the true life. And so too he is the answer to the question of meaning, the question of salvation, the question of life, for this age and beyond the limits of this age. In the language of John's gospel: "I am the way, and the truth, and the life" (Jn 14:6).

So then the Church is maintained in truth, in the truth of the gospel, in the truth of Jesus Christ. The Church does not keep itself in truth. It *is* maintained: by God, through Jesus Christ, in the Spirit.

The Spirit Breathes Where and When He Wills

God, Jesus Christ are not remote from the believer or the believing community. It was always the conviction of the Christian community that God, Jesus Christ are close, are present to the believer and to the believing community. How? Not only through memory. But through the spiritual reality, presence, efficacy of God, of Jesus Christ himself. In brief, God, Jesus Christ are close to the believer, close to the believing community, *in the Spirit,* present in the Spirit, through the Spirit, in fact as Spirit.

"Spirit," the "Holy Spirit," seems for many people a very mysterious figure. What is the *Holy Spirit?* Palpable and yet not palpable, invisible and yet powerful, real as the energy-laden air, the wind, the storm, as important for life as the air we breathe: these are some of the varied ways in which men from very ancient times have imagined the "Spirit" and God's invisible operations. This Spirit is not the spirit of man, his knowing and willing living self. He is the *Spirit of God*, who is rigorously distinguished as *Holy* Spirit from the *unholy* spirit of man and his world. The Holy Spirit is no other than God himself in so far as he is the power and strength of grace gaining dominion over man's mind, man's heart and indeed the whole man, in so far as he is inwardly present and bears witness to himself in the believer and in the believing community.

As God's Spirit however he is also the Spirit of Jesus Christ raised up to God. Thus God's Spirit cannot be interpreted as an obscure, nameless divine force, but is quite unambiguously the *Spirit of Jesus Christ:* as the Lord raised from death to life, Jesus is possessed of God's power, strength, and Spirit so fully that he himself exists and operates in the mode of existence and operation of the Spirit. The risen Jesus acts at the present time through the Spirit, in the Spirit, as Spirit. In the Spirit Jesus is the living Lord, the way, the truth, and the life, the standard for the believer and also for the believing community, the Church. Neither a hierarchy nor a theology nor a fanaticism, seeking to go beyond Jesus—his word, his conduct, and lot—to appeal to the "Spirit," can appeal to the Spirit of Jesus Christ, to the Holy Spirit. Consequently, the spirits—ecclesial and unecclesial, whatever they may be—are to be tested and discerned in the light of this Jesus Christ.

It is therefore clear now that, as Spirit of God and of Jesus Christ for men, he is never man's own potential, but the strength, power, gift, and *grace* of God. He is not an unholy spirit of man, spirit of the age, spirit of the Church, spirit of office, spirit of fanaticism. He is and always remains the Holy Spirit of God who breathes where and when he wills and does not permit himself to be claimed as the justification of absolute teaching and ruling power, of unsubstantiated theology, pious fanaticism, and false security of faith.

The Spirit works *where* he wills. The Spirit of God cannot be restricted in effectiveness by the Church. The Spirit works not only from above but very decisively from below. He works not only in church ministries but where he wills: in the whole people of God. He works not only in the "Holy City" but where he wills: in all churches of the one Church. He works not only in the Catholic Church but where he wills: in the whole of Christendom. And, finally, he works not only in Christendom but again where he wills: in the whole world.

The Spirit works *when* he wills. Certainly, the free Spirit is not a spirit of arbitrariness, of pseudo freedom, of enthusiastic fanaticism, but of true freedom; he is not a spirit of chaos but of order, not of contradiction but of peace: not only in the world but also in the Church. Paul in particular had to insist on this against the Corinthians who appealed to their gifts of the Spirit to justify their neglect of church order: "God is not a God of confusion but of peace" (1 Cor 14:33). Arbitrariness, disorder, chaos in the Church, then, cannot be justified by an appeal to the Holy Spirit.

And yet this does not mean that God's Spirit breathes when he *must*. It is a question of when he wills. No church order in teaching and practice, no dogma and no rite compel him now to act and now not to act. God's Spirit is under no law other than that of his own freedom; under no justice other than that of his own grace; under no power other than that of his own fidelity. God's Spirit therefore is not in any way under the law of the Church, the justice of the Church, the power of the Church. God's Spirit is not governed by the law of the Church, the justice of the Church, the power of the Church. He himself governs and controls supremely the Church's law, the Church's justice, the Church's power. If then anyone in the Church thinks he can possess the Spirit by any means of law, justice, and power, he is bound to fail. The Church does indeed try continually to take over the Spirit, but it cannot "possess" him, cannot control, restrain, direct, or master him.

The Church can do none of these things either by its word or by its sacrament, either by a dogma or by a rite. Certainly God commits himself in the Spirit to the Church's word and sacrament; he does so, however, not in virtue of a law of the Church but in virtue of his own freedom; not in virtue of the Church's justice but in virtue of his free grace; not in virtue of the Church's power but in virtue of his fidelity. Which means that, if he commits himself to the Church's word and sacrament, it is an obligation not for him but for us. It is not we who make demands on him, but he makes demands on us: he requires our unconditional *faith*. Neither the word nor the sacrament operate automatically: if they are not received in faith, they are without effect. If someone thinks he can compel the presence of the Holy Spirit with word or sacrament, or even with law and justice, power and order, he must be lacking precisely in that faith which the Spirit requires of him: the faith, that is, which depends not on his or the Church's justice and law, on his or the Church's power and order, but on God's free grace and fidelity. It remains true then, even in the Church, that the Spirit breathes, not when he must but when he wills.

Could we—we who are the Church—ever forget that

we, though justified, are sinners and are ever freshly aware that we are sinners, that we are consequently opposed to God's Spirit, "grieve" him, and, for our part, may lose him? Could we forget that our faith too, although it gives us certainty, is continually freshly challenged and threatened, that we can only continue to trust in God's fidelity and grace? Is it not clear that we cannot by any means take for granted the *persistence* of the Spirit in us and in the Church? Have we any alternative but to pray continually in a spirit of penance not only, "Come, Holy Spirit," but also, "Remain, Holy Spirit. Remain with us in your fidelity despite our infidelity"? Despite its continual failure in all its members, the Church has not lost the free Spirit of God. This is not something natural, but the miracle of God's fidelity, a fidelity which may not be assumed, but which must be continually believed and sought again in prayer.

Between Traditionalism and Modernism

But has not the Spirit hitherto always guided the Church into all truth? This saying about the Spirit who "will guide into all truth" (Jn 16:13) has often been misused: misused by those who thought they could invoke the Holy Spirit and then be content to leave everything as it was; misused also by those who thought they could invoke the same Spirit and then be able to regard and accept every novelty in the Church as a truth of the Spirit. Both the former and the latter understand the saying in a way contrary to its true meaning.

The former, the slothful *traditionalists* who invoke the Spirit and then defend everything that has become established in the Church, overlook what is said *before* the statement about the Spirit who guides us into all truth: that is, that the Spirit continually comes to "convince the world [and this means the evil, sinful world, hostile to God] concerning sin and righteousness and judgment" (16:8). He comes to judge the world indeed, but also the Church, which is in this world and which only too often appears as a worldly Church. And the Spirit must continually disclose afresh the guilt of this worldly Church. He must open its eyes to sin, justice, and judgment: to sin which is fundamentally unbelief in regard to Jesus Christ, to justice which consists in overcoming through Jesus the world hostile to God, to judgment which has already been passed on this hostile world in Christ's death and resurrection.

The Church too—and this is what we all are—has every reason to ask continually whether it accords with faith in Jesus Christ, whether it lives by his justice, whether it takes account of the judgment that has been passed. The Church has continually every reason for penance and reflection and thus for its own part for conversion, reform, and renewal. Unfortunately, the history of the Church is not a continual ascent, a continual improvement. The idea of perpetual progress even of the Church is an idea of the Enlightenment, not an idea of Christian revelation. In the history of the Church there is a certain progress, but repeatedly also a regress. In the history of the Church there is an ascent, but repeatedly also a descent. In the history of the Church there is a development, but repeatedly also entanglement and aberration.

The Church, believing in the Spirit of Christ who guides it continually into the truth, knows that the Spirit again and again confronts it also with its own sin, with the justice of Christ, and with judgment. It knows that in this very way the Spirit demands of it once more a new faith in Christ, a greater fidelity to the gospel, a life lived more seriously according to his message.

In this sense the Church under the Spirit may never simply leave things as they are, but must continually allow all things to become new in this Spirit who renews the face of the earth and also of the Church, who is the Spirit of him who says, "Behold, I make all things new" (Rev 21:5).

The saying about the Spirit who guides the Church into all truth, however, is wrongly understood, not only by those who think they can appeal to the Spirit to guide them into all truth and then leave everything as it was but also by those who think they can appeal to the same Spirit and then accept every novelty in the Church as a truth of the Spirit. The latter, the superficial *modernists,* overlook what *follows* the statement about the Spirit who guides into all truth: that is, the Spirit who "will not speak on his own authority, but whatever he hears he will speak, and he will declare to you the things that are to come. He will glorify me, for he will take what is mine and declare it to you. All that the Father has is mine; therefore I said that he will take what is mine and declare it to you" (Jn 16:13–15).

What the Spirit then has to tell the Church are not any *new* revelations, *new* teachings, *new* promises, which might be added to supplement or surpass what Christ said. What is said of the Spirit is not that he will guide us into *new* truths, but that he will guide us into *all* the truth. This in fact is the basic conviction of the evangelists, that Jesus' word is the absolutely decisive word which decides life and death. The reason the officers give to the high priest for their failure to arrest Jesus is: "No man ever spoke like this man" (Jn 7:46). The one who speaks here is not one of the Old Testament prophets, whose words are freshly inspired by the Holy Spirit *on each occasion,* but one who speaks and acts *continually* in virtue of his unity with God. No prophet has absolute significance: prophets succeed one another, one comes after the other. But after Jesus there is no new revealer: in him God's revelation is given once and for all to the world.

True, this revelation is inexhaustible. But what is bestowed by the Spirit on the Church as new knowledge does not supplement or surpass what Christ as revealer has said. It is merely the recollection of what Jesus said: the Spirit will only "bring to remembrance" what Jesus said (14:26); he will not speak "on his own authority," but will only say what he "hears" (16:13); he will "take what is mine" (16:14); he will "bear witness" to Jesus (15:26).

The Spirit then will teach *nothing new.* But all that Jesus taught and did he will manifest *in a new light,* in a new age, in the face of new situations and new experiences. Only in this way will the truth of Jesus Christ become freshly clear and intelligible in its meaning for today.

Applications

These more precise definitions should help to make the maintenance of the Church in the truth of Jesus Christ by the Spirit more comprehensible.

1. If remaining in the truth is essentially a question of discipleship in the Spirit of Jesus Christ, this is *more*

a matter of orthopraxy than of orthodoxy: it is realized more in the Christian life than in teaching, more in the deed than merely in the word.

For although what a person believes about Jesus Christ is by no means irrelevant, although this belief must determine his practical approach, it is nevertheless not the ultimate decisive factor. Merely saying "Lord, Lord" is of no avail. The brother who says he will not obey and yet does so is preferred to the one who says he will obey and yet does not. In the passages on Jesus' calling of his disciples he never asks first for a profession of faith. The profoundly disturbing Sermon on the Mount is centered not on orthodox belief but on radical observance of God's will in service to one's neighbor. Why? Because Christian truth is concrete. According to Matthew, at the last judgment the verdict depends on what is done, on involvement on behalf of one's fellow human beings.

2. If remaining in the truth is essentially a question of discipleship in the Spirit of Jesus Christ, this is *a matter more of individuals and individual communities than of institutions.* Obviously Christian institutions also are bound by the gospel of Jesus Christ. But institutions as such cannot guarantee the persistence of the believing community in truth.

Because institutions are in the hands of men, they can be misused and corrupted. Often the individual and the individual community are maintained in the truth of Jesus Christ, despite the failure of certain institutions and their representatives to function evangelically (and therefore call for reform). However much institutions are necessary for a community and so too for a believing community, and particularly for a large believing community, in the last resort they are not essential for persistence in truth. They should foster this permanence, but may also prevent it. The Church is essentially a believing community, but decisions for faith occur in the heart of the individual. Institutions have no heart. There is an ultimate immediacy of the individual to God and to his truth over which no institution has power, not even by means of the stake or of excommunication. Discipleship of Christ therefore is continually possible even when it is more impeded than helped by institutions.

3. If remaining in the truth is essentially a question of discipleship in the Spirit of Jesus Christ, this is manifested *not only in the great, strictly orthodox churches but also among heretics.* This does not mean that heresy thus becomes truth. Whatever represents "another gospel," thus rendering doubtful the foundation of the faith of the ecclesia and consequently opposed to the ecclesia, cannot be described as truth. But if we look at concrete individuals and communities, this distinction between truth and error is by no means easy to establish.

This is so because, on the one hand, there is truth in heresy: genuine heresies live not so much by error as by the truth invested in them and often exaggerated. On the other hand there is also error in the Church: errors, aberrations, and deceptions, omissions, blockages, and displacements, have often provided an occasion, a cause, an opening, for heresy. The latter often did not represent arbitrary action but understandable reaction: in good faith, in faith in the gospel, in the determination not to betray that gospel. Good faith, even good faith in Christ, must not be denied to the heretic. Errors may be condemned, but not erring individuals. Even

the heretic can be influenced and can abide by the gospel and has been so influenced, often more than the
self-important highly orthodox individual. It is because
of this faith that discipleship of Christ is by no means
impossible for him. Hence it must be said that, as the
Church is preserved in the truth despite all errors, the
heretic who strives for discipleship in virtue of his faith
in the gospel is similarly preserved despite his heresy
(which is not on that account justified).

4. If remaining in the truth is essentially a question
of discipleship in the Spirit of Jesus Christ, this is manifested, *despite the failure of hierarchy and theology, in the
living faith of the "little people."* There were times when
little of the truth of the gospel could be observed in the
lives and activities of hierarchs and theologians, when
the Church came close to perishing and the promise of
indestructibility seemed an empty phrase. But when
popes and bishops pursued power, money, and pleasure, and theologians kept silent, slept, produced apo-
logias, or even collaborated, there still remained those
innumerable, mostly unknown Christians (among them
at all times even some bishops, theologians, and particularly parish priests) who tried even at the worst times
of the Church to live according to the gospel.

Thus it was not so much the high and mighty, the
clever and wise, but the "little people," the "insignifi-
cant," who—and this is wholly in accordance with the
New Testament—were "witnesses of the truth" and
manifested the indestructibility of the Church. That
genuine renewal, which for the most part was not at-
tained by any sort of dogmatic definition but by reflection on the gospel, by a change of awareness and genuine repentance, in prayer, suffering, and action, came

very often and at first unobtrusively from the circles of these "little people."

Under these circumstances what function is left to the various offices in the Church, especially those which provide a service, for the persistence of the Church in truth? Here we can only draw some provisional conclusions from what has been said. In any case offices do not establish truth in the Church. Officeholders too can err and frequently do err and, like institutions generally, can be corrupted. Officeholders therefore are not the cause of the Church's persistence in truth. It is despite the error even of many officeholders that the Church is maintained in the truth. The gospel itself is the source, norm, and power for faith and for the continuity (perenniality) and indestructibility (indefectibility) of the believing community in the truth. Of course officeholders can and should have a positive, auxiliary function in this respect, in so far as they have to undertake in particular a service to the *truth* in the light of the special function of each office in the service of the gospel and of the believing community. As far as the Church's leaders are concerned, this is a service to the truth by the manifold proclamation of the gospel and the meaningful administration of the sacraments publicly before the congregation and consequently by active commitment in Church and society.

We shall have to return to this question. But before that we must discuss another aspect of maintaining the Church in truth: the concrete problem of errors in the Church.

Chapter 3

Living with Errors

Errors Are Facts

In the course of discussions on infallibility people often
ask with some anxiety what would happen if the
Church, if a Pope or a council, were to err with reference to an important question of faith or morals in a solemn definition which would formerly have been
regarded as infallible.

The question is understandable. What happens in the
event of error? First of all the answer must be that there
is no need at all for panic. Error on the part of the
Church's magisterium in serious definitions of faith or
morals is in any case a fact—and we are still alive. If
anyone thinks that *Humanae vitae* is not sufficiently
clear or serious, let him consider the definition of the
Council of Trent on the transmission of original sin
through procreation or the definition of the same council (which cannot be justified in the light of Christian
origins) on the sacramental character of ordination as
an indelible mark on the soul. Or, again, what about

the solemn condemnation (understood in a dogmatic sense) of freedom of religion and conscience or the solemn proclamation in church documents from the time of the Galileo crisis up to our own century of the complete inerrancy of the Bible? We need not discuss here when an "infallible" definition was involved and when it was not (this is a distinction introduced subsequently). According to Vatican I and II, the "infallibility" not only of the "extraordinary" but also of the "ordinary," everyday teaching of Pope and bishops, extending to a variety of things, would have to be considered. In any case, even in the past century, quite a number of statements were presented as articles of faith (*de fide*) which are not admitted today (we need only recall the condemnations of the *Syllabus of Errors* of Pius IX which were regarded by some theologians after Vatican I as "infallible," the theses against the scientific theory of man's origin, the antimodernist professions of faith required of all the clergy under pressure of conscience and compulsory oaths).

But whatever may be or may have been considered in particular as "infallible" teaching and what was not, there is a consensus on the fact of an erring magisterium even with regard to the organs of "infallible" dogmatic definitions (Pope, episcopate, ecumenical council). And the errors involved were certainly sufficiently serious in themselves and in their consequences. For many this is now evident in the case of *Humanae vitae*. Obvious also today more than ever are the negative consequences of the Augustinian theory of original sin as transmitted by procreation, consequences in regard to the disparagement of sexual pleasure and in regard to the salvation of unbaptized chil-

dren; the consequences also of the doctrine of the sacramental character (likewise going back to Augustine)
for dogmatically justified clericalism; of the doctrine of
the inerrancy of the Bible for the Church's attitude to
the natural sciences and history; of the condemnation of
freedom of conscience and religion for many persecuted
Protestants and for the position of Catholics in modern
society.

Any minimizing of the errors of the ecclesiastical
magisterium is out of the question. Nevertheless . . .

The Church Lives On

In the believing community, as with conflicts, we must
live or learn to live with errors. The Church has "sur-
vived" errors or "survives" them up to a point in the
immediate present with some pain. But it continues to
live and, despite all the serious encumbrances, the truth
can be perceived in the Church now as before. For in
the last resort the Church does not live by its errors but
by the truth of the gospel, which is able to prevail even
alongside numerous and serious errors.

To be more precise, there can be discipleship of
Christ even if a believer understands one or another
point of doctrine in a way that is contrary to the gospel.
A truly evangelical basic attitude can be no more nullified by individual erroneous propositions than it is by
individual sins. Correctly understood, "simultaneously
justified and sinner" (*simul justus et peccator*) has its parallel in a rightly understood "simultaneously believer
and unbeliever" (*simul fidelis et incredulus*). Every believer has reason to confess, "Lord, I believe, help my
unbelief!"

What is true of the individual can be said analogously of the ecclesial community. In the Church there will always be a sufficient number of people who so live according to the gospel that the message can be perceived and that to speak of the ecclesial community remaining in the truth makes sense, a permanence in the truth which cannot be nullified by individual erroneous propositions even if these have an official character. Like the *simul justus et peccator*, so too the *simul fidelis et incredulus* has an ecclesiological dimension. The Church is not a community of the perfect; it is on pilgrimage, *in statu viatoris*. More important than one or another false step, one or another wrong turn or detour, is the basic trend, determined by promise, of the believing community in the truth and toward the ultimate truth, which itself—as we have stressed—is a truth of faith. All detours and wrong turns in wandering through the desert did not in any way alter the fact that the ancient people of God were basically on the right road to the promised land. All the false steps, false conclusions, blunders, and slips will not ultimately divert the people of God now wandering through many a desert from its destined course.

Even a possibly false dogma (and how many a dogma has been forgotten today or touches the Christian's sense of faith marginally at best) cannot destroy the Church's being and truth. The totality of faith consists in the integrity of commitment, not in completely correct propositions. And that commitment can be entire and unreserved even though something false is said at the same time. Errors of the Church's magisterium are a serious matter, but they are not a threat to the existence of the Church. This is precisely what is meant by the promise of indestructibility in truth. And this promise should really take away from Christians of little faith that fear of error which often appears to be greater than the fear of sin. Why does not the Holy Spirit prevent such errors from the outset? This was the kind of question raised by a number of people before and after *Humanae vitae*. The answer is that God's Spirit does not nullify man's humanity: to err is human. The more urgent question is why the Church in particular, which has written reorientation and repentance on its banner, has notable difficulty in correcting its errors. The answer is that the Church is inclined to identify itself with God's Spirit and thus ascribes to itself God's infallibility, from which it then deduces the irreformability, the incorrigibility, of its definitions. Should not the opposite be the case? Should not the Church under the gospel, as *ecclesia semper reformanda*, revise and correct its errors more easily and more rapidly than others and in this very way render credible precisely its indestructibility in truth.

If then we are to allow so concretely for errors on the part of the Church's magisterium, how can we know at all what is truth in the Church and what is not? The problem of *confirmation*, of *verification*, arises here.

Chapter 4

Criteria of Christian Truth

The Gospel of Jesus Christ as Primary Criterion

The first thing to be noticed is that recent teaching on infallibility is faced with quite serious difficulties when it comes to verification. Even if I accept infallible propositions as a fact, the question arises as to why these statements are true. Certainly their truth does not simply follow from their infallibility. Even according to the usual teaching, dogmas are not true because they have been defined; they are defined because they are true. Why then are they true? Why, for instance, is the dogma of Mary's immaculate conception supposed to be true, but not the dogma (desired at least by some people) of the immaculate conception of Saint Joseph? The more radical question might be: Why cannot both be true or both false?

What then is the *criterion* to be if we have to allow for errors on the part of the ecclesiastical magisterium and, under certain conditions, even in what were formerly regarded as infallible dogmatic definitions?

Certainly it cannot simply be practice: otherwise success would become the criterion of truth and what is there that is not successful in this world?

Neither can it simply be reason: otherwise Christian truth would be reduced to general truths of reason and thus become superfluous.

But it cannot be the faith, or the sense of faith, of the people: otherwise it would become only too often superstition.

Finally, the dogmas themselves cannot form the criterion: this would be to beg the question, an argument which turns out to be a vicious circle (dogmas are true because they have been made into dogmas).

The method of verification must be appropriate to the facts to be verified. There are various forms of verification. The criterion for what is supposed to be true in the *Christian* Church can be nothing but the *Christian message,* the gospel of Jesus Christ as originally recorded in the New Testament—in writing, making arbitrary changes and developments impossible—and thus *Jesus Christ* himself. The New Testament (as explained in concrete detail in *On Being a Christian*) may not be understood in a biblicist-fundamentalist sense as a collection of infallible statements, but must be given an historical-critical interpretation at the highest level of modern hermeneutics. At the same time it must be transmitted to the present, not only existentially with respect to the individual but also socially with respect to the community, a process in which practice in the second place has also a hermeneutical function: how far can this truth have its influence on life?

The Significance of the Community and Tradition

Since Christian truth does not claim to be an eternal idea but is essentially historical truth, there are two factors which cannot be neglected in the process of verification.

The first is the factor of *community*. This truth reached me by way of the believing community and is still lived today in that community. Whether I want to do so or not, I cannot disregard this sociological context. But since I am part of that living, believing community itself, from which these testimonies have emerged and to which they continue to mean life, I could gain a deeper understanding of the meaning of these testimonies both originally and today.

The second factor is *tradition*. The Christian message was not devised by the present generation. It has been handed down through a history of twenty centuries. I am neither the author nor the first interpreter of Christian truth. History, like the community, can help me to break through the limits of my subjectivity and to perceive the truth more deeply and more comprehensively. The community and the tradition of the Church then form an essential part of the process of discovering Christian truth. This is precisely what is meant by catholicity in space and time.

The Christian and in particular the theologian is thus siutated at a point between the original gospel and the present-day ecclesial sense of faith. Anyone who simply accepts as "super-criterion" either the "Church's present sense of faith" or the ecclesiastical "magisterium" in one way or the other becomes an apologist for the ecclesiastical system: he is overlooking the fact that, even according to Vatican II, the magisterium is under the word of God and consequently is open to criticism in the light of the normative criterion of Scripture. On the other hand, anyone who neglects the Church's sense of faith and simply makes the gospel the ultimate criterion is in danger of lapsing into an emotional subjectivism: with the aid of the historical-critical method he makes light of the ultimate authority of faith. It seems as if a hermeneutical circle cannot be avoided in practice. Unlike the historian of religion, the theologian works within the limits of the Church's faith and presupposes it, but at the same time is expected to study it in a critically scientific spirit. In this respect he or she resembles up to a point the political theorist who is loyal to his state and the constitution and yet has to study it in a critically scientific spirit. This is difficult, but not impossible.

A critically scientific theology is therefore required and not a theology which is part of the "system," justifying the Church's dogmatic system in every case. The theologian who works in this way from within the system starts out from the "Church's present sense of faith" or, more precisely, from the "infallible" official ecclesiastical dogmatic definitions and continually returns to these definitions. Since it is claimed that the latter can never have been false and therefore may not be corrected under any circumstances, only two possibilities remain: either simply to repeat them and support them with any quotations from Scripture and Tradition that can be found (this is how positive neoscholastic theology works) or to "interpret" them speculatively and try to make it possible for them to be

assimilated by the modern mind (this is how specula-
tive neoscholastic theology works). Since such an "interpretation" lacks any sort of criterion, no limits are set
in practice to subjective whim in this "interpretation"
or "re-interpretation" of dogmas. Thus the axiom "Outside the Church no salvation" is still used today when it
is admitted by Vatican II that vast numbers of people in
no way attached to the visible Church can be saved, so
that it means in effect: "Outside the Church there is certainly salvation." Interpretation is turned into contradiction.

On the other hand, the critically scientific theologian
takes account quite concretely of the Church's sense of
faith—and not only the present but also the former
sense of faith (catholicity in space and time), which, as
shown in the question of papal and conciliar infallibility, often includes a critique of the actual sense of
faith. This present-day sense of faith must on no account be justified at the expense of truth. It must be
measured against the original, authoritative New Testament testimony of faith and, under certain conditions,
be very substantially corrected.

Hence various theological *loci* or sources of theology
must certainly be considered, but they are not to be ar-
tificially harmonized, assimilated, and equalized, as if
they were all of equal value! No, all ecclesiastical decisions, even the most solemn conciliar ones, on their
own admission never possess more than a derived, sec-
ondary *standardized authority* by comparison with the
original, primary *standardizing authority* of the gospel
and Jesus Christ himself who is attested there. It is then
only with reference to the gospel of Jesus Christ—to
which they always seek to appeal—that councils and

other ecclesiastical authorities can demand an unconditional assent. This is also true if it is assumed that councils cannot err, but it becomes even more important if
the possibility of error is admitted.

In What Does the Christian Believe?

What does the Christian actually believe in? Not in
propositions certainly, nor precisely in truths (in the
plural). It is true that professions of faith, which sum-
marize certain truths or events, can be helpful; but the
Christian does not believe "in" professions. Definitions
of faith, which mark off certain points of the Christian
message from what is unchristian, are perhaps unavoidable in extreme situations; but the Christian does not
believe "in" definitions. Strictly speaking, he does not
believe "in" the Bible or "in" tradition or "in" the
Church. But the specific danger of Protestant belief in
particular is biblicism, the danger of Eastern Orthodox
belief is traditionalism, and the danger of Roman Catholic belief is authoritarianism. All these are defective
modes of belief. On the other hand, it must be clearly
stated:
• The Christian (even the Protestant) believes, not in the
  Bible, but in him whom it attests.
• The Christian (even the Orthodox) believes, not in
  tradition, but in him whom it conveys.
• The Christian (even the Roman Catholic) believes, not
  in the Church, but in him whom it proclaims.
The absolutely reliable reality, to which man can cling
for time and eternity, is not the biblical text, nor the
work of the Church Fathers, neither is it an ecclesiastical magisterium, but it is *God himself as he has spoken*

and acted for believers through Jesus Christ. The texts of
the Bible, the statements of the Fathers and of ecclesiastical authorities—in varying importance—are meant to
be no more and no less than an expression of this faith.

Consequently, I do not simply believe various facts,
truths, theories, or dogmas: I do not believe this or that.
Neither do I believe merely in the trustworthiness of a
person: I do not believe simply in this person or that.
What I do is to venture to commit myself quite per-
sonally to a message, a truth, a way, a hope, ultimately
to someone: I believe in God and in him whom God has
sent.

All of this should have brought out the ultimate reason why individual articles of faith are important but
not in the last resort decisive. Certainty, dependability
and assurance are conveyed—through all the propositions—by the ground of faith: God himself and his
Christ, who is proclaimed in propositions, in true propositions, but who is able also to rouse attention by am-
biguous and occasionally even false propositions.

Faith is like *love.* If I love someone but have to explain suddenly why I love that person, I may stutter,
make mistakes, exaggerate one thing and understate another, say something distorted or even false, stress what
is unimportant and even forget what is important. But
this is not necessarily detrimental to my love. Love is
dependent on statements if it is to find expression. But
love is not completely expressed in statements. True
love persists even through untrue statements.

It is the same when I have to say why I *believe* in God,
in Jesus. I formulate my reasons perhaps obscurely, im-
precisely, even falsely. I overlook one thing and over-
value another. In my statement I may miss what is abso-

lutely essential and have to correct myself afterwards. But this need not be detrimental to my belief in God and Jesus. Belief is dependent on propositions if it has to be professed, expressed, proclaimed, taught. But faith is not completely expressed in propositions. True faith is maintained even through untrue propositions. Christian faith is not a closed, quasi-mathematical system of propositions, as a theology infected with rationalism tried to make it, so that it ceases to be true as soon as one of the propositions is found to be incorrect (hence up to a point the anxiety to make sure that all propositions are correct). Christian faith, like love, can be wholly real, even if one of its propositions is not correct.

Is this not a consoling answer? Very much more consoling than the promise at some point of a number of guaranteed, infallible propositions, which still could not save us. If, following Augustine, we say, "Love, and do what you will," we could perhaps analogously say, "Believe, and say what you can." This second brief statement is at least as misleading as the first: the importance of good and true formulations of belief should not be played down. But the essential point should be made clear, that to those who love God (and men) all things— even distorted and false formulations of faith—eventually work for good.

Chapter 5

The Opportunities
of a Fallible Magisterium

Is the Magisterium Incapable of Functioning?

The task of the Church, of each individual, and especially of the leaders, is to bear witness to this faith of theirs and give an account of it, to hand on the good news in word and deed, to make clear the grandeur of the cause of Jesus Christ and so too the grandeur of the cause of God and of man, to explain and interpret the meaning of all this quite concretely for modern man and modern society. In this sense there is really no objection to a (pastoral) magisterium, even though the term, introduced at a late stage and not clear in its connotation, is better avoided, since it suggests an anonymous bureaucracy (particularly if we speak of a "Teaching Office" as a kind of parallel to a "Home Office" or a "Foreign Office") and implies an unbiblical distinction between the Church teaching and the Church taught.

47

It would be better to speak concretely of leaders and heads of churches and congregations, of parochial clergy (in the widest sense, as including parish priests, curates, and chaplains) and bishops (including the Pope). These leaders and heads of the local, regional, and universal Church have as their great, primary task to see to the proclamation of the gospel publicly before the Church and the world. At the same time the greatest importance is to be attached to the daily, and in particular Sunday, proclamation event, compared to which any kind of solemn, extraordinary acts (a single "infallible" definition, for instance, in a hundred years) are much less significant. These church leaders should undertake their function of leadership mainly through the daily proclamation of the gospel in a variety of shapes and forms, assisting, encouraging, exhorting, and consoling: they should lead their congregations, large or small, in the spirit of Jesus Christ, they should work on individual believers and groups, integrating, coordinating, stimulating, inspiring, and eventually also representing the community internally and externally. In this sense we can speak of a *ministry of leadership and proclamation on the part of priests and bishops* (as also of the Pope).

Here however the question repeatedly arises as to whether the magisterium is rendered *incapable of functioning* (incapable of action, checkmated) if it cannot produce any infallible decisions. How are the Pope, the episcopate, the council to undertake their task if in a case of doubt they cannot define infallibly who is right? How, that is, can they function without infallibility? In the first place, of course, we can answer that Pope and bishops are continually exercising their function, even though they produce "infallible" decisions only in the rarest cases (parish priests, incidentally, produce none at all). There can be no question therefore of paralyzing their magisterium if they are denied the power of making infallible decisions. Instead, such a denial implies a positive invitation to them to take even more seriously their fundamental, normal, daily task of proclamation. Nevertheless, we must go briefly into the question of how episcopate (in council) and Pope can function if, like the ordinary priest, they cannot make infallible decisions.

In this connection one thing must be mentioned first. Oddly enough, as the discussion on infallibility has shown, people today scarcely seem to have any difficulties with the fallibility of the *Bible* like those which they have with the fallibility of the Pope or of a council. The Bible anyway functions quite well even without infallible propositions. After all the difficulties with modernism, eventually even with Rome's consent, the historical-critical method came to prevail in Catholic exegesis much earlier than in Catholic dogmatics, where that which has long been taken for granted in the exegesis of the Bible is only now being realized in the history of dogma: truly historical thinking. In historical-critical exegesis it has been shown that the truth of Scripture is not only not destroyed but even emerges with fresh clarity and luminosity when at last we cease to defend every statement of Scripture as infallibly true because "inspired." A wholly fresh light was thrown on the great truth of a good God and his good world in the creation account when the attempt was abandoned to establish for apologetic reasons a concordism, with every statement regarded as true in the scientific or historical sense. Even without infallible statements, the Bible was thus able to assert its unsurpassable authority, to make effective its absolute claim to truth, to offer continually a new invitation to faith and radical commitment.

How the Council Might Function

If the Bible can manage without infallible propositions, the question naturally arises of whether councils likewise might function without them? How is the infallibility of councils to be substantiated by Scripture if the latter itself shows no signs of possessing such infallibility?

   If we want to see concretely how councils can function without infallible propositions, it is best to take a look at the first ecumenical council, that of Nicea in 325, which managed without making any claim to infallibility. Recent historical investigation has brought out how Athanasius, the leading person at this council, together with the Greek Fathers and also Augustine, established the true, although by no means infallible, authority of a council. A council tells the truth not because its convocation is legally unimpeachable, not because the majority of the bishops of the world are gathered there, not because it is confirmed by any human authority, not because it has the extraordinary assistance of the Holy Spirit, and not because it cannot then be a priori deceived. No, despite the new words, a council does not tell new truths; but it tells the truth because it conveys the old tradition in a new language, because it attests the original message and breathes Scripture, *because it has the gospel behind it.* Why could not a council function in this way even today?

Oddly enough, the first and what is currently the last ecumenical council of the Catholic Church coincide in this respect, that neither wanted to produce definitions which would be a priori infallibly true. The infallible definitions at first envisaged by the curial preparatory theological commission of Vatican II would have been about as much or as little use as Pius IX's long list of condemned errors a hundred years earlier. John XXIII, less as a theologian than as an evangelically minded pastor and man of common sense, had seen that infallible decisions would be of no advantage to the council, that the council would function only if it was *pastorally oriented, giving new currency to the truth of the gospel*, without any claim to infallibility, in the language of people today. As he said in the opening speech to the council, "The salient point of this Council is not a discussion of one article or another of the fundamental doctrine of the Church which has repeatedly been taught by the Fathers and by ancient and modern theologians, and which is presumed to be well known and familiar to all. For this a Council was not necessary." What the Pope expected was an up-to-date proclamation: "a step forward toward a doctrinal penetration and a formation of consciousness in faithful and perfect conformity to the authentic doctrine, which, however, should be studied and expounded through the methods of research and through the literary forms of modern thought." To those who fear modernism in any reorganization and renewal of doctrine the Pope points out, "The *substance* of the ancient doctrine of the deposit of faith is one thing, and *the way in which it is presented* is another. And it is the latter that must be taken into great consideration with patience if necessary, everything being measured in the forms and proportions of a magisterium which is predominantly pastoral in character."*

A council then can be of service to Christian proclamation, albeit only to a limited extent (without professional theology) and at best when concentrated on certain important points. It will normally be able to undertake this *theoretical task* credibly only if it works at the same time for the *practical renewal* of the Church in the Christian spirit. The Council of Nicea itself (this fact is often overlooked) was occupied also with questions of church discipline. And in the tradition of the high medieval reform councils, both at Trent and at Vatican I and II "reform," together with "teaching," became the second pole of the conciliar efforts. Quite frequently the success or failure, the functioning or nonfunctioning of a council has been measured more by its results by way of reform than by the effects of its teaching.

All this does not exclude the possibility that a council may produce unambiguous demarcations, not indeed in any questions of theological detail but wherever essential Christian values are at stake, in extreme cases. But even then (the history of the "reception" or "acceptance" of councils by the ecclesial community proves this) the council will prevail, not by claiming ecumenicity or infallibility (many councils have tried to do this in vain) but only because and in so far as it has the truth of the gospel credibly behind it. A council then can speak only in a way that relates to the particular situation and not by any means infallibly, but nevertheless *with binding force* and in decisive questions with ul-

*"Pope John's Opening Speech to the Council," in Walter Abbott (ed.), *The Documents of Vatican II* (New York: Herder and Herder/Association Press, 1966; London: Geoffrey Chapman, 1966), p. 715.

timate binding force. This ultimate binding force can come only from the truth behind which is God himself: from the Christian message which, in a particular situation, does not permit long discussion and careful differentiation, but can demand a completely sincere and absolute assent (on certain occasions as a matter of life or death).

When a child has fallen in the river, we do not discuss the different methods of saving life. If it is really a question of the existence or nonexistence of the Church or if the fate of innumerable human beings is directly involved, theological distinctions are out of place and a clear profession of faith must be attempted, even though this might be dangerous. It is of course understood that eventual condemnations must arise out of a real emergency and at some cost to the ecclesiastical representatives; they should not be facile interventions of ecclesiastical bureaucracies in times of peace, seeking to stifle instead of accepting justified criticism. As protection against accidents does not constitute the sum total of children's education, neither does proclamation in the Church consist merely in the condemnation of errors. The *opportunity* of a council today, as Vatican II showed very clearly, lies in making a constructive contribution, without any claim to infallibility and in full awareness of the limited possibilities, to the solution of the great problems of the Church, of Christendom, of society, and of humanity today.

How the Pope Might Function

How could the Pope function without infallible dogmatic definitions? In our own time we have seen something of both possibilities. First there was Pope Pius

XII, who decided a century after Vatican I to claim the authority ascribed to the Pope by the council but not claimed in the meantime, in order to proclaim *urbi et orbi* an infallible dogmatic definition, a new Marian dogma. And yet none of his dogmatic statements were so disputed in Christendom and even in the Catholic Church as this "infallible" definition. The pastoral effects on the devotion of the Catholic people and the conversion of the world, expected at the time, are seen in a more sober light at a distance of thirty years. Vatican II dissociated itself from extreme Marian ideas and in practice brought these to an end, making even more obvious the dubiousness of that definition.

The other example is of the next Pope, John XXIII, who from the very beginning had no intention of pronouncing an infallible definition. On the contrary, he repeatedly insisted in one form or another on his own human weakness, limitation, and even from time to time on his fallibility. He lacked the aura of infallibility. And yet none of the Popes of this century exercised a greater influence on the course of the history of the Catholic Church and indeed of Christendom as a whole than did this Pope who attached no importance to infallibility. With him and Vatican II a new epoch of church history was inaugurated. Without any infallible propositions he succeeded in gaining a hearing once more in a variety of ways for the gospel of Jesus Christ in the Church. Consequently he possessed an authority inside and outside the Catholic Church which would have been unthinkable in the time of his predecessor. Anyway, with all his weaknesses and faults, more spontaneously than deliberately, more symbolically than programmatically, he let it be seen in outline how the Pope might be really Pope without any claim to infallibility. Such a Pope would not jealously insist on his powers and prerogatives or exercise authority in the spirit of the ancien régime, but would exercise an authority of service in the spirit of the New Testament related to the needs of the present time. He would enter into fraternal partnership, cooperation, dialogue, consultation, and collaboration, especially with the bishops and theologians as a whole; he would involve those concerned in the decision-making process and invite them to share responsibility. The Pope then should exercise his function in this way even in questions of proclamation and teaching: *in* the Church, *with* the Church, *for* the Church, but not *above* or *outside* the Church.

Again, there is nothing to prevent a Pope from occasionally reacting *against* something and under certain conditions being bound to react. No infallible decision would have been required, a clear understandable word in terms of the Christian message spoken by Christ's "Vicar" would have sufficed in the face of the invasion of Poland or the mass murder of the Jews. It is strange however that nothing was said "infallibly" in recent times at the very moment when countless people might have expected it. On the other hand, despite all fallibility, the Pope (together with the rest of the bishops) can serve the ecclesial community and its unity, inspire the Church's missionary work in the world, intensify its efforts for peace and justice, for disarmament, human rights, the social liberation of peoples and races, its involvement on behalf of the underprivileged of all kinds. Without any claim to infallibility, as mediator and inspirer in the Spirit of Christ and as leader in the Christian renewal, he can constantly make the voice of the

Good Shepherd heard in his teaching and working in the Christian *oikumene* and far beyond it. Rome would thus become a place of meeting, for discussion and for sincere and friendly collaboration.

Out of all this it follows that the Pope can function even without infallible dogmatic definitions; indeed, under the present conditions of Church and society, he can fulfill his ministry *better* without infallible dogmatic definitions. If anyone therefore questions papal infallibility in regard to propositions, he is not thereby questioning the papacy as such. So much must be said emphatically against constant confusions, distortions, and suspicions. There is a good deal about the Petrine ministry that has become questionable, especially the medieval and modern absolutist forms which have been maintained up to our own time. A Petrine ministry has a future only if it is understood in the light of the Petrine symbol in the New Testament. The exegetical and historical substantiation of an *historical* succession of the bishops of Rome has become questionable. But a Petrine ministry has retained its objective meaning if, in its *functional and practical* succession, it is a ministry to the Church as a whole: a *primacy of service* in the full biblical sense.

Such a primacy of service, as it became visible at least in outline in the person of John XXIII, offers a real *opportunity* to the Catholic Church and to Christendom as a whole. A primacy of service would be more than a "primacy of honor": the latter cannot be condoned in a Church of service, nor in its passivity can it be a help to anyone. A primacy of service would also be more than a "primacy of jurisdiction": the latter is a complete misunderstanding if it is taken to mean sheer power and authority; literally understood, it conceals the very essence of this primacy, the aspect of service. Petrine ministry, understood biblically, can only be a "pastoral primacy": a pastoral ministry to the Church as a whole. As such and regardless of all unclarified and indeed unclarifiable questions of *historical* succession, it is supported objectively by the New Testament. In this sense it could be of the greatest value today for Christendom as a whole. It would speak for the great concerns not only of Roman Catholic Christianity but of Christendom as a whole.

Chapter 6

In Case of Conflict

Different Functions

It should be clear by now that the ministries of leadership can function as a service of pastoral proclamation without infallibility. We withdraw nothing of what has been said, we do not weaken but in fact strengthen authority, if, again on the lines of Vatican II, we stress the fact that the ministries of leadership must act continually in collegiality, solidarity, and fellowship with all *other ministries* in the Church. No one in the Church has a monopoly of truth; no one may limit, channel, or regularize the diverse charisms.

Among these other ministries, from the very beginning, "prophets" and "teachers" in the Church have had a special importance which cannot be superseded by the ministries of leadership. Prophets and theologians in particular are at the service of truth in the Church.

The *prophets*, lesser or greater, men or women, aware of their vocation and responsibility, by letting the Spirit speak directly in a particular situation point the way to the present and the future. Their "one-sided" warnings and "harsh" demands on the Church and its leaders— like those of the Old Testament prophets in regard to the hierarchs and the people of Jerusalem—are unwelcome at the time, but they also convey courage, clarity, and joy for the renewal of the truth by the power of the Spirit.

The *theologians*, for their part, struggle by different methods to find the authentic tradition and the correct interpretation of the original message, in order to bring the latter out of the past and offer it freshly to Church and society today. By critical scrutiny of current teaching and reflection on the gospel itself they can stimulate and inaugurate better proclamation and action.

And what happens when *conflicts* arise over the question of truth in the Church, conflicts especially between leaders and teachers in the Church, between bishops (or Pope) and theologians? Here we can offer only a few brief observations.

On Coping with Conflicts

1. Conflicts are *borderline cases*. In determining the authority of church leaders and theologians and their relations with one another, we must not think simply in terms of a case of conflict and in that light try to establish the dominion in principle of one group over the other. The case of conflict must remain a *borderline case*; it must not be allowed to become a basic model. Here too fear is a bad counsellor.

2. Even in the Church conflicts are *unavoidable*. They are signs of life and in any case are to be preferred to

the deathly silence of totalitarian systems. Conflicts must be endured and a fruitful settlement attempted. At the same time no group may simply outmaneuver the other. It is no help to the well-being of the whole or the freedom of the individual if one group comes to prevail at the expense of the other; instead there must be intensive and active collaboration in the service of the common cause.

3. A solution in principle for cases of conflict, which are always possible, must be based on the clearest possible *differentiation of areas of competence*. Obviously even this will not lead to an idyllic future for the Church, free from conflict. But by the clear demarcation of responsibilities and with moderation on the part of each group many conflicts could be avoided from the very beginning. Leaders on the one hand and theologians on the other have their own specific charism, their own peculiar vocation, their proper function. Theologians should not want to be bishops nor should bishops want to be theologians. Neither a church of professors nor a church of hierarchs accords with the New Testament. Both the ministry of leadership of bishops and priests and the ministry of teaching of theologians have their particular importance and also their particular assumptions. From the outset they are dependent on one another's cooperation, since they both have their origin in the same gospel of Jesus Christ and both exist for the same people. Both have to serve the proclamation of the gospel in their own specific fashion, whether by leadership (preeminently by preaching at the congregational act of worship) or by study and teaching.

4. We cannot discuss here in detail how churches are

to be governed or the study of theology pursued in a normal situation. What is *essential* for church leadership and theology is laid down in the *gospel*. More is left to human regulation than is generally assumed. Normally, for instance, councils in the Catholic Church are convoked according to the rules of canon law; from the middle ages the task of convocation has been assigned to the Pope. But this is a question of human law. The possibility of convoking a truly universal council of all Christian churches should not be excluded because of questions of law and protocol.

5. While allowance has to be made for the clear demarcation of responsibilities between the functions of church leaders and theologians, in an emergency under certain conditions the one group must undertake in a subsidiary fashion the functions of the other. When church leaders fail, theologians must talk and act; when theologians fail, church leaders must do the talking and acting. Here everyone—obviously also the lay person— has his own responsibility which he cannot pass on to anyone else. Whenever, as a result of the failure of one group or the other, it is a question of the existence or nonexistence of the Church of the gospel, then a *status confessionis* exists, then people cannot be content to be merely spectators. Then some will have to come to the aid of the others, in order resolutely to do what they can to serve the believing community.

6. Genuine emergencies and emergency situations are such that they cannot be foreseen or *settled in advance* in their concrete shape. Who is to extinguish a fire can be planned in advance only up to a point. When the fire actually breaks out, the person who happens to be available will deal with it, even if he does not belong to

the fire department. This is not a plea for abolishing or neglecting the fire department. In an emergency, regardless of questions of legal competence, each and everyone must do what is necessary. In church history there are plenty of examples of subsidiary action of one group for the other. Bishops reacted to a disastrous and dangerous confusion on the part of theologians in questions of faith (in the ecumenical councils of the first millennium). Bishops and theologians acted when the Popes failed to do so (as in the Great Schism of the West and the reform councils). Pastors and lay people rallied round a theologian of the Confessing Church when Catholic and Protestant bishops and the Pope failed to take action (in regard to National Socialism in Germany).

7. Despite the possibility of distinguishing them in principle, the *frontiers* between the different areas of competence are *fluid* in the individual case and cannot always be clearly defined. In particular, in the individual case, it is not easy to discover whether it is a question of the existence or nonexistence of the Church, whether this question or that is merely a question of theology or really of faith. From the very outset theologians will have to guard against subjectivistic enthusiasm and church leaders against doctrinaire authoritarianism and both against obstinacy. It is not a state of emergency when a curate or teacher of religion in a parish does not speak about the resurrection or the divinity of Jesus with that exact orthodoxy which a theologian or bishop or episcopal theologian might expect in the light of his dogmatic theology. A state of emergency exists in a church when *preaching and action are continually and unambiguously contrary to the gospel.* The es-

sential norm for judging the situation is not some view-point of ecclesiastical politics, but the gospel itself. The subsidiary intervention of one group for the other is permissible only as a last resource. A state of emergency may not simply be presumed as a reason for intervention either by church leaders or by theologians. In the first place, in a spirit of self-criticism, all other possible ways and means must be used.

In view of all the unforeseeable, incalculable, and un-controllable conflicts in the Church, a trust emerging from belief in the indefectibility of the Church is partic-ularly important and the development and application of imagination is a real Christian virtue if aid is to be provided for every emergency. Creative imagination can consider models, methods, and solutions, can make clear how difficult situations may be managed—even without infallible propositions and authorities. In this way do we not need to be less fearful for the future of the Church?

Chapter 7

In Conclusion

Looking Back

The indestructibility of the Church of Jesus Christ as the whole community of believers is itself a truth of faith, rooted in Christian origins, based not only on isolated classical texts but on the Christian message as a whole, which as God's final decisive call will continue to awaken belief and to assemble a community of believers. The conviction of believers from the very beginning was that the Church is maintained quite concretely by God in the truth of Jesus Christ wherever his Spirit, the Holy Spirit of God, is alive and continually bringing fresh guidance into the whole truth; wherever, that is, Jesus himself is and remains the way, the truth, and the life for the individual or for a community; wherever people commit themselves in discipleship to his way; wherever they follow his guidance on their own way of life. Consequently this persistence in truth is more a matter of orthopraxy than of orthodoxy, more a matter of individuals and individual communities than of institutions. With the ever-possible failure of hierarchy and theology, this persistence in truth continues to be manifested in the living faith of "little people" and in fact, not only in the great churches, but occasionally outside these. Here it becomes especially clear that the ecclesiastical ministries do not establish truth in the Church, but are there to serve it and men.

The result is that the Church continues to live even in the event of serious error in a matter of faith or morals, indeed that the Church must continually be learning to live with errors. Errors of the ecclesiastical magisterium are a serious matter, but they are not a threat to the existence of the Church. The Church however needs a criterion for what is to be considered as true in the Christian Church: this is the Christian message as originally recorded in the New Testament, ultimately Jesus Christ himself. This Christian message must be read critically against the background of the ecclesial community and tradition. Precisely in this way it becomes clear that the Christian ultimately believes not in propositions or truths, not even in the Bible, in tradition, or in the Church, but in God himself and in him in whom God revealed himself. Such a faith is indeed dependent on propositions if it is to be expressed, but it need not be destroyed by false propositions.

Hence both the everyday and the extraordinary proclamation can be sustained despite individual errors. In particular it can be made clear that episcopate, council, and Pope can function and undertake their task even though in a case of conflict they cannot define infallibly who is right. In this way it is even easier to cope with cases of conflict, which are always possible in the Church.

Looking Forward

A fallible magisterium would then have to be seen as an opportunity. Could not the *Church of the future* cope with its errors more easily in this way? That is, it could learn by its mistakes, using the method of trial and error advocated by Karl Popper. Would this not be a way of regaining the old freedom to secure a hearing for the truth of the gospel again and again throughout all the errors? If sin could become a "happy fault" (*felix culpa*), might not error also (in itself much less serious) become a "happy error" (*felix error*), since the truth of the gospel shines out all the more brightly through the Church's errors? Could not church history be considered more realistically in this way and yet at the same time belief in the persistence of the Church in truth become more convincing?

A consensus in the direction outlined is possible and seems to be emerging in various publications. It would be an *ecumenical consensus*, for in this way other Christians too could believe in the indestructibility, the indefectibility, of the Church of Jesus Christ in truth. The most serious impediment between the Christian churches would thus be removed. But more importantly, the Christian message, this Jesus himself and the God for whom he stands, would have become more credible again. And for that alone the pursuit of theology is worthwhile in the troubles of the present time.

Does not what has been expounded here deserve to be freshly considered? Following the French theologian *Yves Congar*, one of the great precursors of the Second Vatican Council, in this matter so serious for the Catholic Church and Christendom and also for himself, the theologian may be permitted to put forward a plea:

Let the question of infallibility be freshly investigated—now, under a new Pope—in objective relevance, scientific honesty, fairness, and justice.

Let an ecumenical commission—on the lines of the commission on birth control in the sixties—composed of internationally recognized experts from the various disciplines (exegesis, history of dogma, systematic theology, practical theology, and the nontheological studies also involved), be appointed to look into this question.

Let there be less importance attached to the negative-critical approach than to the positive-constructive one, and then let the question be asked whether the *persistence of the Church in truth, despite all errors,* is not better substantiated in the Christian message and the great Catholic tradition and whether it would be better to live with this even in the Church today.

After the rejection of any kind of contraception by Pope Paul VI—justified, in the Roman view, by the authority, continuity, traditionality, universality, and consequently in practice by the infallibility and irreformability of the traditional teaching—it might be hoped that a solution of the question of infallibility would carry with it also a solution of the question of contraception. What for countless people in our developed countries with their declining birth rate represents a serious burden of conscience means for the people in many underdeveloped countries, and especially in Latin America, incalculable harm, for which the Church must share responsibility: poverty, illiteracy, unemployment, undernourishment, and sickness are related to high birth rates as effect to cause. During the past two decades the growth rates of food production (by no means slight) were largely outpaced by the higher birth rates.

Pope John Paul II returned from Latin America with new experiences. There he had spoken out against poverty, underdevelopment, and child misery. In view of all this and in light of the fact that he wants to work for ecumenical understanding, is it too much to expect from him a decisive step toward an honest clarification of the pressing question of infallibility—in an atmosphere of mutual trust, free research, and fair discussion?

Postscript to the
Original Edition

This theological meditation is not intended to provoke
a new controversy on infallibility. The most recent debate,
which can now be seen at a certain historical distance,
has brought out a number of things:

1. No one—neither a theologian nor an ecclesiastical
authority—has been able to produce a proof of guaranteed infallible propositions, and the blind alleys to
which infallible propositions lead are today more evident than ever (see *Fehlbar? Eine Bilanz,* edited by Hans
Küng [Zurich: Benziger, 1973]).

2. The ecclesiastical authorities have taken scarcely
any notice of the negative result of the debate; they
repeated with slight modifications only the magisterial
utterances which had been called in question (see the
various declarations of the Roman Congregation for the
Doctrine of the Faith and of the German Bishops Conference in 1973 and 1974).

3. A constructive Catholic theology, which does not
start out from within the system, from certain defined

propositions only to return to them, but which can make the original message of God and his Christ freshly effective for us today, is possible (see the author's *On Being a Christian* [New York: Doubleday, 1976; London: Collins, 1977] and *Does God Exist?* [to be published in 1980 by Doubleday and Collins]).

4. The questioning of the traditional teaching on infallibility continues even within the Catholic Church and in Catholic theology (see the recent book by August E. Hasler, *Wie der Papst unfehlbar wurde: Macht und Ohnmacht eines Dogmas* [Munich/Zurich: Piper, 1979]).

But the debate about infallible propositions and authorities is not to be continued here (I made some observations on the subject in a preface to Hasler's book). What ought to be done is to process the positive conclusions of the infallibility debate (which have been too little considered) and then, without polemics, to explain how today a persistence of the Church in truth can be believed and understood (see the last chapter of *Fehlbar? Eine Bilanz*). The majority of thinking people today are not concerned as to whether error can be a priori excluded as a result of the assistance of the Holy Spirit (infallibility of individual propositions or authorities) in certain cases (in practice, extremely rare today). But in view of the new problems assailing the Church in the first, second, and third worlds, in view of the numerous ideologies of the left and right, a much more fundamental question arises: whether a persistence in truth can be ascribed to the Church at all or whether this Church and its truth are not coming to an end. The question then is no longer the infallibility of certain ecclesiastical statements of faith and authorities on faith, but the indefectibility of the Church itself.

The French theologian Yves Congar has called for a *re-reception of the papal dogmas of Vatican I*. Congar, who contributed more than anyone to the theological preparation of the new understanding of the Church presented by Vatican II, thinks that the historical relativity of Vatican I has been brought home most effectively by a number of historical studies (Aubert, Torrell, Schatz), by works on the history of theology (Thils, Dejaifve, Pottmeyer) and those that raise radical questions (Küng), also by the very fact of Vatican II and the revival of local and partial churches, and finally by the new understanding of the principles of Eastern ecclesiology. He has called—"in our Catholic loyalty"—for a "re-reception" of the Vatican dogmas and especially the dogma of papal infallibility. According to Congar, keeping in mind a genuine understanding of the magisterium, the best exegetical, historical, and theological studies of recent decades, the ecumenical dialogue inaugurated under new conditions, the theology and reality of the local Church, there should be a fresh reflection together with the other Christian churches and a new formulation of what was defined at Vatican I in 1870 and was then accepted by the totality of Catholics in the relativity of that period. According to Hasler, such a re-reception in practice would lead to a *revision* of the decisions of Vatican I, which would provide the Catholic Church and Catholic theology and Christendom as a whole with a way out of a situation that has become untenable into a new future. But, once again, we have no desire here to provoke a new controversy on infallibility; what ought to be done is to liquidate the old controversy as soon as possible. Hence our suggestion of the appointment of an ecumenical commission.

Postscript to the English Edition

WHY I REMAIN A CATHOLIC

On December 18, 1979, the Sacred Congregation for the Doctrine of the Faith issued a "Declaration on Some Major Points in the Theological Doctrine of Professor Hans Küng." The Declaration accused Professor Küng of having departed in his writings from "the integral truth of the Catholic faith" and pronounced that "he can no longer be considered a Catholic theologian nor function as such in a teaching role." In particular, Küng was charged with "contempt for the magisterium of the Church" on the issue (among others) of papal infallibility, as expressed most recently in Kirche—gehalten in der Wahrheit? (The Church—Maintained in Truth). What follows is Professor Küng's response.

Why do I remain a Catholic?

This is not an easy question to answer in the midst of a time- and energy-consuming controversy, when it becomes almost unbearable to write at all. After an unjust and unfair procedure on the part of the highest ecclesiastical authorities, I was deprived by decree of the title of "Catholic theologian" and an attempt was made to drive me out of my faculty of Catholic theology after 20 years of teaching there and to thrust me—without being overscrupulous about methods—to the margin of my Catholic Church very shortly after I had completed 25 years as a priest and celebrated my jubilee. In the face of harassments and threats, is it possible to offer declarations of loyalty or to make professions of faith?

Under these circumstances, why do I remain a Catholic? From thousands of letters, telegrams, telephone messages, the same depressing question faces me, raised in sadness, anger, and despair in a variety of ways by innumerable Catholics throughout the world. Many are wondering if the wheel of history is to be turned back in our Catholic Church to the time before John XXIII and the Second Vatican Council. Are the new openmindedness, readiness for dialogue, humanist and Christian spirit again to yield to the triumphalism disavowed by the Council? Are Roman authorities again to abolish the freedom of theology, to intimidate critical theologians, and to be allowed to discipline them by the use of spiritual power? Are bishops to be merely recipients of orders and to be obliged to enforce the Roman policy on those who are under their care? And, despite fine ecumenical words and gestures, is the ecclesiastical institution with its unecumenical attitudes and deeds to become once more an unfriendly, inhospitable, unfruitful "fortress" in this modern society of ours?

This latest development has in fact driven some already to formal secession from the Church and very many more to definitive internal emigration. This indeed is the most disastrous feature of the present ecclesiastical policy: The silent mass withdrawal from the Church will continue. And particularly those who as pastors, curates, and teachers have to dole out what the hierarchs have cooked up for them—that is, those who are looking helplessly for arguments to make the Roman measures intelligible in response to people's critical questions—will want to know the answer to the question "Why remain a Catholic?"

A Personal Question

It is not any liking for theoretical problems which makes me raise this question, but the necessity of defense. For the doubts about catholicity are not mine, they are raised by certain authorities and hierarchs. Why then do I remain a Catholic? For me as for many others the answer must be first of all that I will not allow anyone to deprive me of what has been valuable and dear to me throughout my life. I was born into this Catholic Church: baptized, it is true, into the much larger community of all those who believe in Jesus Christ—nevertheless, born at the same time into a Catholic family which is dear to me, a Swiss Catholic parish to which I am always glad to return: in a word, into a Catholic homeland which I do not want to lose, which I do not want to abandon. All this I feel precisely as a theologian.

At a very early stage, I became acquainted also with Rome and the papacy, and—despite all calumnies—I do not cherish any "anti-Roman feeling." How often am I to continue saying and writing that I am not against the papacy nor am I against the present Pope, but that I have always contended inside and outside the Church for a Petrine ministry—purged however of absolutist features—on biblical foundations! I have continually spoken out for a genuine pastoral primacy in the sense of spiritual responsibility, internal leadership, and active concern for the welfare of the Church as a whole: a primacy which might then become a universally respected authority for mediation and conciliation in the whole ecumenical world. It would of course be a primacy not of dominion but of unselfish service, exercised in responsibility before the Lord of the Church and lived in unpretentious brotherliness. It would be a primacy, not in the spirit of a Roman imperialism with religious trimmings, such as I came to know quite closely under Pius XII during my seven years of study in Rome, but a primacy in the spirit of Jesus Christ, as it was illustrated for me in the figures of Gregory the Great and John XXIII (as a theologian at Vatican II I was able to observe him at close quarters). These were Popes who expected not servile submissiveness, uncritical devotion, sentimental idolization, but loyal collaboration, constructive criticism, and constant prayer on their behalf: collaborators of our joy, not masters of our faith, to adopt a saying of the Apostle Paul.

At a very early stage, too, I came to know the Catholic Church as embracing the whole world and in it I was able to receive and learn an immense amount from innumerable people—many of them friends—everywhere. From that time onward, I have become more clearly aware that the Catholic Church must not become confused simply with the Catholic hierarchy, still less with the Roman bureaucracy.

But above all there was Tübingen, Protestant Tübingen with its Catholic faculty. Here as professor from 1960 onward, I have increasingly become a part of this faculty which, from its foundation, has had a great history, not only of success, but also of conflict. How many Catholic theologians in Tübingen, including some who are still alive and teaching, have been admonished, put on the Index, harassed, and disciplined! There is nothing new under the Tübingen sun.

It was from this Catholic faculty of Tübingen, in the free air of Tübingen, that both my books and the books of my colleagues emerged and without which they would scarcely have been possible or at any rate only in another form. In continual discussion with colleagues and students it was possible for a Catholic theology to emerge here, which—unlike the former controversial theology—has a truly ecumenical character and seeks to combine two things: loyalty to the Catholic heritage and openness to Christendom—in fact, to the ecumenical world as a whole. Discussion, particularly with Protestant colleagues, was of decisive importance, not in order to disparage the Catholic reality, still less to squander it, but in an ecumenical spirit to throw new light on it from the gospel and to gain a deeper understanding of it. Seeing this task as my duty, I was able in 1963 to switch over in the Catholic theological faculty to the recently established chair for dogmatic and ecumenical theology. This position was combined with the direction of an Institute of Ecumenical Research which worked systematically for the convergence of divergent theologies without attempting to avoid questions hitherto regarded as taboo. Under these conditions, can a theologian be blamed for defending himself with all legitimate means against the pressure to get him out of this faculty of his?

Why then do I remain a Catholic?

Not merely because of my Catholic *origins* but also because of this *life task* of mine which is grasped as a great opportunity and which as a Catholic theologian I can fulfill appropriately only in the context of the Tübingen faculty of Catholic theology. But now the question must be asked: What, properly speaking, is this Catholic reality for the sake of which I want to remain a Catholic theologian?

Who Is a Catholic Theologian?

In accordance with the original meaning of the word and with ancient tradition, anyone can describe himself as a Catholic theologian if he is aware of being obliged in his theology to the "Catholic"—that is, to the "*whole*," the "universal, comprehensive, total"— Church. This catholicity has two dimensions: temporal and spatial.

First, *catholicity in time:* A theologian is Catholic if he is aware of being united with the whole Church—that is, with the Church of all times. He will therefore not describe from the outset certain centuries as "un-Christian" or "unevangelical." He is sure that in every century there was a community of believers who listened to the gospel of Jesus Christ and tried in one way or other, so far as it is possible for human beings in their frailty and fallibility, to live according to his example.

Protestant radicalism on the other hand (not to be confused with evangelical radicality) is always in danger of wanting unhistorically to begin at zero and so to pass from Jesus to Paul, from Paul to Augustine, and then in a great leap to pass over the Middle Ages to Luther and Calvin, and from that point to leap across one's own "orthodox" tradition to the more recent church fathers or, better, heads of schools.

The *Catholic* theologian, by contrast, will always start out from the fact that there was never a time when the gospel was left without witness and he will try to learn from the Church of the past. While insisting on the necessity of critical scrutiny, he will never overlook the boundary posts and danger signals which the Church in former times, in its concern and struggle for the one true faith, often at times of great distress and danger, set up in the form of creeds and definitions to distinguish between good and bad interpretations of the message. He will never neglect the positive and negative experiences of his fathers and brothers in theology, those teachers who are his older and more experienced fellow students in the school of sacred Scripture. It is precisely in this critical scrutiny that the Catholic theologian is interested in the *continuity* which is preserved through all disruptions.

Second, *catholicity in space:* A theologian is Catholic if he is aware of being united with the Church of all nations and continents. He must therefore not orient himself only to the church of this country or to a national church and will not isolate himself from the Church as a whole. He is sure that in all nations and on all continents there is a community of believers who in the last resort want nothing other than their own church, a community which is driven no less than the local church by the gospel and which itself has something to say for this local church and its theology.

Protestant particularism on the other hand (not to be confused with evangelical congregational attachment) will always be inclined to orient itself to the locally restricted church, its faith, and its life, and to be content with a theological (occasionally intellectual, highly cultivated) provincialism.

The Catholic theologian will always start out from the fact that the gospel has not left itself without witness to any nation, any class or race, and he will try to learn from other churches. However deeply rooted he may be in a particular local church, he will not tie his theology to a particular nation, culture, race, class, form of society, ideology or school. Precisely in his specific loyalty, the Catholic theologian is interested in the *universality* of the Christian faith embracing all groups.

It is in this twofold sense then that I want to be and remain a Catholic theologian and to defend the truth of the Catholic faith in Catholic depth and breadth. And there is no doubt that a number of those who describe themselves as Protestant or evangelical can be and are in fact catholic in this sense, particularly in Tübingen. There ought to be joy at this, even on the part of the institutional Church.

The Criterion of What Is Catholic

Does this affirmation of what is Catholic in time and space, depth and breadth, mean that you have to accept more or less *everything* that has been officially taught,

ordered, and observed in the course of twenty centuries? Is it such a total identification that is meant by
the Vatican Congregation for the Doctrine of the Faith
and the German Bishops Conference when they speak
of the "complete," "full," "uncurtailed" truth of the
Catholic faith?

Surely what is meant cannot be such a totalitarian
conception of truth. For, even on the part of the institutional Church, it is now scarcely disputed that momen-
tous and even theologically "justified" errors have oc-
curred in the history of Catholic teaching and practice
and have been corrected (most tacitly) up to a point
even by the Popes. The list is immense and includes the
excommunication of the Ecumenical Patriarch of Con-
stantinople and of the Greek Church, prohibition of
vernacular liturgy, condemnation of Galileo and the
modern scientific world-view, condemnation of Chinese
and Indian forms of divine worship and names of God,
the maintenance of the medieval secular power of the
Pope up to the First Vatican Council with the aid of all
the secular and spiritual means of excommunication,
condemnation of human rights and particularly freedom
of conscience and religion, and discrimination against
the Jewish people; finally, in the present century, the
numerous condemnations of modern historical-critical
exegesis (with reference to the authenticity of the books
of the Bible, source criticism, historicity, and literary
genres) and condemnations in the dogmatic field, especially in connection with "modernism" (the theory of
evolution, understanding of development of dogma);
and, in very present times, Pius XII's cleaning-up measures (likewise dogmatically justified) leading to the
dismissal of the most outstanding theologians of the

pre-conciliar period such as M. D. Chenu, Yves Congar, Henri de Lubac, Pierre Teilhard de Chardin, who almost all became conciliar theologians under John XXIII.

Is it not obvious that a distinction must be made, precisely for the sake of what is truly Catholic? Not everything that has been officially taught and practiced in the Catholic Church is Catholic. Is it not true that catholicity would harden into "Catholicism" if that which has "become the Catholic reality" (the words are those of Joseph Cardinal Ratzinger of Munich) is simply accepted instead of being submitted to a criterion? And for the Catholic Christian too this criterion can be nothing but the Christian message, the *gospel* in its ultimate concrete form, *Jesus Christ himself,* who for the Church and—despite all assertions to the contrary—also for me is the Son and Word of God. He is and remains the norm in the light of which every ecclesiastical authority—and this is not disputed—must be judged: the norm by which the theologian must be tested and in the light of which he must continually justify himself in the spirit of self-criticism and true humility.

All this means that to be "Catholic" does not imply—for the sake of a supposed "fullness," "integrity," "completeness," "uncurtailedness"—a false humility obediently accepting *everything,* putting up with *everything.* That would be a fatal pooling of contradictions, a confusion of true and false.

Certainly Protestantism has often been reproached for accepting too little, for making a one-sided selection from the whole. But on the other hand, it is often impossible to avoid reproaching Catholicism for accepting too much: a syncretistic accumulation of heterogeneous, distorted, and occasionally un-Christian, pagan elements. Which is worse: a sin by defect or a sin by excess?

In any case then Catholicity must be critically understood—critically, according to the gospel. Together with the Catholic "and" there must be considered the repeatedly necessary protest of the "alone," without which the "and" can never be meaningful. Reforms—in practice and teaching—must remain possible. For the theologian, this means nothing other than the fact that the Catholic theologian in a genuine sense must be evangelically oriented and conversely that the evangelical theologian in a genuine sense must be oriented in a Catholic way. Admittedly, this makes the theological demarcations objectively and conceptually more complicated than they might seem to be in the light of official doctrinal documents which are often terribly simple and display little catholic depth and breadth. Why then do I remain a Catholic? Precisely because as such I can assert an "evangelical catholicity" concentrated and organized in the light of the gospel, which is nothing but genuine ecumenicity. Being Catholic, then, means being ecumenical in the fullest sense.

But what of the Roman factor?

"Roman Catholic" is a late and misleading neologism. Once again, I have nothing against Rome. I mean that precisely because I wanted to be a Catholic theologian, I could not tie my Catholic faith and Catholic theology simply to the ingrown Roman absolutist claims from the Middle Ages and later times. Certainly, there must be development in doctrine and practice, but only an *evolutio secundum evangelium,* or "a development in accordance with the gospel." An *evolutio praeter evangelium,* or "a development apart from the gospel," may be tolerated. But an *evolutio contra evangelium*, "a development contrary to the gospel," must be resisted. Applied to the papacy, this means that I have always acknowledged and defended the pastoral primacy of the Bishops of Rome linked to Peter and the great Roman tradition as an element in Catholic tradition that is supported by the gospel. But Roman legalism, centralism, and triumphalism in teaching, morality, and church discipline, dominant especially from the 11th century onward, but prepared long before then, are supported neither by the ancient Catholic tradition nor—still less—by the gospel itself; they were also disavowed by the Second Vatican Council. On the contrary, these things were mainly responsible for the Schism with the East and with the Reformation churches. They represent the "Catholicism" about which the present controversy is being carried on in the name of the catholicity of the Catholic Church.

Are there some of our cardinals and bishops who do not want to see that in individual points of theory and practice their thinking is more Roman than Catholic? Perhaps my Protestant colleague, Walther von Löwenich, an authority on both Luther and modern Catholicism, has rightly seen this in the infallibility debate when he writes: "The essential question in the Küng case is not appropriately stated as 'Is Küng still a Catholic?' It should be, 'Will Catholicism struggle out of its dogmatic constriction into genuine catholicity?' "

Catholicity then is gift and task, indicative and imperative, origin and future. It is within this tension that I want to continue the pursuit of theology and as decisively as hitherto to make the message of Jesus Christ intelligible to people of the present time, while being ready to learn and to be corrected whenever it is a question of discussion between equal partners in a fraternal spirit. I must insist, against all the repeated assertions to the contrary by the German bishops, that I have never refused such a discussion even in regard to the Roman authorities, and that I have frequently had this kind of discussion both with representatives of the German Bishops Conference and with the local bishop. But, for the sake of protecting human and Christian rights and for the sake of the freedom of theological science, I have had to resist throughout all the years an interrogation of an Inquisition according all rights to itself and practically none to the accused person. That much I owe to those also who have suffered—and, as it seems, will suffer in the future—under these inhumane and un-Christian measures.

Catholic Church, yes! Roman Inquisition, no!

I know that I am not alone in this controversy about true catholicity. I shall fight against any acquiescence together with the many people who have hitherto supported me. We must continue to work together for a truly Catholic Church that is bound by the Gospel. For this, it is worthwhile to remain a Catholic.

St. Paul's Clifton
Bray Library